STUDIES IN FRENCH LITERATURE No. 1

General Editor
W. G. Moore
Fellow and Tutor of St. John's College, Oxford

RACINE: BRITANNICUS

by
W. G. MOORE
Fellow and Tutor of St. John's College, Oxford

BARRON'S EDUCATIONAL SERIES, INC.
Great Neck, New York

Printed in the United States of America

Contents

General Preface

This series of volumes is designed to illustrate an experimental approach to the classics of a foreign literature. All will agree, I think, that such classics are not difficult to obtain, in a reliable text, but that much of the material that accompanies modern editions could be dispensed with. We do not go so far as to suggest that a student should be confronted with a 'plain text' and left to supply such commentary as he can. This would be a clear waste of many people's time. Teachers and students are much too busy to dig out relevant material each for himself. Literary study is as complicated as any other science. It has its methods, old and new, and its tools. We have aimed in this series at discarding outworn tools and supplying new ones. We give no biographical material, save where a fact sheds light on a feature of the work. We exclude all that does not seem to be immediately helpful for the understanding of an actual text, whether it be historical background, glossary or quotation. We assume that our readers possess the usual manuals, dictionaries and of course the text of the work to which we aim to introduce them.

The space thus made available we have used to present and discuss the evidence needed to appreciate a work of literary art as an aesthetic creation. We think that every student should be made aware, as too many are still not made aware, that a work of art is not a copy, nor a sermon; that it is never the same as any or all of its sources; that its value never consists in the moral truths it may contain. We approach famous works of art as attempts to make something, to construct a pattern. We consider them as the result of both vision and talent. Remembering that we were told much of the talent and little of the vision we have tried to redress the balance. We have kept in mind that a work of art seems to be, and never is, perfect, just because it aims to do 'something unattempted yet'. We hope without superiority to suggest points at which the artist was defeated, for these show up the range and power of his achievement. We have tried to put ourselves in the position of the artist confronting his subject, in fact to follow the advice of a master of French studies:

> Qu'il s'agisse d'un roman, d'une pièce de théâtre, d'un poème, placez vous au point de vue de l'auteur, réalisez le problème technique qu'il s'est posé, calculez les résistances de sujet et les ressources du génie, introduisez ses modèles, supposez ses moyens, ré-inventez ses combinaisons: je ne prétends pas que votre tâche sera facile et sans risques, mais vous avez chance de renouveler la critique d'un ouvrage sur lequel tout semble avoir été dit. En serrant de plus près le processus de la création vous couperez à la racine des erreurs d'interprétation dont autrement il est bien difficile de se défaire.

In order to attain this rather ambitious objective, we have tried to reduce the gap between writer and reader, to appeal directly to the judgement of the student, to leave decisions to him, to allow him to disagree with, or to question, our putting of the case. We hope that teachers will make use of the opportunity to bring the pupil into a discussion, rather than to impose as authoritative our, or their, reading of a work. We would welcome reactions to what we have written.

We do not wish to claim that these introductions are 'all our own work'. We have recalled, with a gratitude which we would here and now express, points that we owe to our own teachers, to the works of many scholars and editors, to colleagues, and above all to our students who were the guinea-pigs of the views we here express, and whose questions have taught us as much as we can have taught them.

W. G. M.

Introductory

When you are about to open the text or see the curtain rise on this play, you stand before the experience of a highly complex work of art. Your enjoyment will therefore depend on your familiarity with the conventions observed in it, and on your understanding of what the poet is trying to convey to you. Both these things are easier for the French than they are for us. We are accustomed to a dramatic tradition in which the conventions are concealed: we like 'realism', which means the illusion of 'the real thing'. *Britannicus* is a perfect example of something very different, which means that once you have mastered the medium you can have a new kind of enjoyment. And to master the medium you do not need great learning. You need to be alert, unprejudiced, ready to take the spectacle (or the text) on its merits. To judge it by anything else is to prejudge it, and will in the end leave you disappointed.

This is a French play about Roman history. To grasp it, you need no great knowledge either of Roman or of French history, but it may help you to learn a little about the society in and for which it was written. It is, as you know already, nearly three hundred years old. It was first performed in Paris on December 13th, 1669. Its audience, which included Corneille, would be a cross-section of middle- and upper-class society, very much like Restoration society in England, people like Pepys and those who appear in his Diary. The year 1669, as it happens, was the year in which the last pages of the Diary were written, the year in which Rembrandt died in Amsterdam. (He would have liked the sombre colours and mysterious subject of *Britannicus*, similar to his own pictures.) It was in Paris the year of *Tartuffe*, the year of the death of Henrietta Maria of England, whose husband, Charles the First, had been executed in Whitehall twenty years before. While writing his play Racine possibly went to a convent by the Seine (where the Palais de Chaillot now stands) to hear Bossuet's funeral oration on the Queen.

The play was not an immediate success. We know that its first performance was spoilt by a public execution: many people preferred to go to see the Marquis de Courboyer beheaded (a commoner would have been hanged) than to go inside a theatre. Racine seems to have had the critics against him, as so many of the best French writers have had: Corneille before him, Flaubert and Baudelaire and Proust after him. The only surviving account of the first performance is hostile, and rather silly. But more and more people saw that here was something important and in a preface to a second edition after seven years Racine could write: 'Les critiques se sont évanouies, la pièce est demeurée.' In the same preface he revealed the fact that of all his plays (that is before *Phèdre*) he had spent most time and trouble on this one. It soon became recognised as a marvel of classical art, and I shall try to give you now and then some of the things that French critics and scholars have said in admiration of it. For the moment a single testimony from our own day may be enough to suggest that you are not wasting your time. Paul Claudel, the poet-statesman, once said that he was unable to find a single flaw in what he called 'le sévère et sculptural premier acte de *Britannicus*'.

1. The Kind of Play

Britannicus is classical drama, a product of the period the French look back on as their great age, their 'splendid century' (a readable book by Mr. W. H. Lewis has this title). When we say classical French drama we speak of a peculiar kind of play, which grew up in certain medieval monasteries on the model of the plays of Seneca. French Renaissance poets recommended and revived it and thence up to Racine's own day it had been steadily getting more popular. A great dramatist, Pierre Corneille, had made it for thousands of French people into an elegant entertainment, so that 'going to the theatre' became quite the thing for middle-class people. By 1650 there were three regular theatres in Paris where this elegant drama could be seen three afternoons each week. These were the theatre in the Marais district where Corneille's plays were mostly given, one in the Palais Royal where Molière had established a company, and (the oldest and most 'stylish' of all) one in the Hôtel de Bourgogne, where *Britannicus*, like *Andromaque* before it, could be seen. All these, by the way, were rectangular halls, not circular theatres like the Greek or the English. This meant that the audience was not around but in front of the stage, and looked beyond the

actors to a perspective of conventional classical scenery. The
first stage setting of *Britannicus* was as follows: 'Théâtre est
un palais à volonté'. All this made for a certain kind of drama
and had perhaps more influence than we have hitherto
thought on the type of play that Corneille and Racine were
asked to supply.

The most obvious mark of this kind of play was declamation. Its appeal was to the ear even more than to the eye.
There was little scenery, no changes of scene, no expensive
costumes (actors wore a queer compromise of ancient and
modern robes), but the great thing was the speeches. They
were all in verse and were recited in a sing-song tone more
like chanting than speaking. (You may study, if you are
interested, Molière's dislike of this custom and his effort to
convey tragedy in a more natural voice. It was a complete
failure.) We are told that long speeches by the main actors
went down well and kept the house quiet, but that minor
parts could often hardly be heard. So actors demanded from
authors fine bombastic speeches that would give them a
chance to show off. The chanting and the high-flown language had been a part of the play from its medieval begin-
nings. One early document says that the whole idea of tragedy
is to 'convey in noble song the fall of a great house'. Noble
song, that is, as far as possible from prose, from the everyday,
from realism. (Make sure that the things you dislike about this
drama are not exactly the things it aims at doing: if you want
it to be like real life, when it is concerned to be unlike real
life, no wonder you will not get the point.) Noble song, the
fall of a great house, misfortunes of princes . . . all this is in a
way the subject of *Britannicus*, and all this Racine and his

generation had taken over from Corneille, as Corneille had taken it over from earlier dramatists like Hardy and Garnier, and they in their turn from the monasteries. Classical drama is just as medieval in origin as the mystery plays, but it is a different kind of tradition.

The declamation has been modernised but the style cannot be. You and I must get used to it. As far from prose as possible, the opposite of 'vulgar' in all senses. The key words are not ordinary words, as in Shakespeare, but stilted and pompous words. (The French word 'pompeux' is a term of praise and means grand.) Look how Burrhus tells the Empress not to get excited (829) or how Nero refers to the death of his father (1654). The language does not aim at realism: it is deliberately artificial. This is not an extra, it shows how people thought of tragedy, as an august thing, the reverse of mean and ordinary. (Remember that ordinary life was much more mean in that age than it is for most of us.) A performance of tragedy kept even in the 17th century something of a religious rite, of something to be chanted with dignity rather than reported with accuracy.

This feeling was so strong that early French classical tragedy is for us impossibly unreal and high-flown. Indeed, it only became a popular box-office entertainment after the encouragement of Richelieu and the emergence of a group of gifted modernising playwrights (Corneille, Mairet, Rotrou, Desmarets, Tristan) had shown how to bring in natural expressions and appealing human reactions alongside the grand style; this sort of thing:

Rodrigue, as-tu du cœur?
— Tout autre que mon père l'éprouverait sur l'heure.

This was fascinating, in its complete and delicious sense of shock, to a generation that had wearied of old-style tragic laments and prophecies and bombast. Corneille indeed is Racine's great master in the introduction of the natural along-side the elevated. His lines were so brilliant and so popular because they had the force of epigrams and yet seemed sayable and realistic. Let us take another case so that you may become familiar with the rhetoric inherited by Racine. Two soldiers before combat:

1. Albe vous a nommé, je ne vous connais plus.
2. Je vous connais encore, et c'est ce qui me tue.

These are ordinary words but grand attitudes, and so elemental, yet so complete in definition, that Pascal made a note of them as perfect descriptions of what could be called the human and the inhuman way of looking at things.

The same sort of judicious mixture of the artificial and the prosaic makes the charm of Racine's tragic style. Some of his lines make you wonder, others sound just like a living person speaking prose. And this mixture was what his audiences loved. Their lives were rough and harsh (as Aldous Huxley has wonderfully shown), reading was rare and the theatre was interesting for those who could not read, or who disliked reading, as much as for those who could. Other current entertainment was gross and unpleasant. But here in the modernised serious play was tense interest, fine speech, an inside view of 'the great', how they talked, plotted, killed and were killed. Such a mixture to a people such as the French, who have always loved drama, was irresistible. The charm has lasted for over two hundred years.

2. Intellectual Spectacle

Declamation was the keynote, but it was not the only attraction. Everything else was in keeping: no fisticuffs or brawls on stage; not physical action but feeling, reaction, all that goes on in the mind or between friends, prior to action: dilemmas, surprises, change of mind, risk, scandal. We might put it this way and say that in this drama the deed was less interesting than its preparation, or its reception. In Livy's story the great thing is the fight between Horatii and the Curiatii, but in Corneille's play this event has little importance. The emotional reactions in a single family before and after it, these are the subject. Corneille's subject is really not Livy's subject at all, although Livy gave him the setting and the background. His Parisian contemporaries were not interested in seeing a poor copy of a Roman fight: they had more stirring stuff at their own street corners. But they were very much interested in warlike emotions, in the risk of invasion, in saving the country and in military psychology, for at the time of the play, in 1640, France was at war and men had gone from home to fight. Corneille in *Horace* and similar plays showed how Roman history could be used to illustrate contemporary attitudes. As we shall see, the lesson was not lost on the young Racine.

At this point, and before you get down to actual study of the play, you might well exercise your powers of historical imagination and try to picture what playwrights like Corneille and Racine were really trying to do. As I was taught French literature, they were concerned to observe a set of specially-drawn-up rules, in particular the three unities: it was because

he could not 'violate' (as the term was) the unity of place that
Corneille was prevented from showing Livy's actual battle.
This way of looking at French drama was, I now think,
doubly wrong. It attached too much importance to dramatic
critics and it made matters much too simple. For a paid
dramatist in the Paris of 1660 matters were not simple at all.
The first people who had to be satisfied were the public. Plays
that did not draw a full house would not be paid for. This
meant that the plays that succeeded did so, not because certain
pundits approved, but because they provided considerable
dramatic entertainment. The plays that have become classics
of the stage have continued to supply this entertainment to
successive generations. This should make us pause before we
criticise what may not be to our taste, but what has been
admired, and over a long period of time.

But the author had to please not only his public but his
actors. He knew who would say his lines and what sort of
lines the actor or actress would say best. It was a single actor
who often made the success of a play. Parisians of 1637 did
not say: 'You must see *Le Cid*, the first real classical play.'
They said: 'You must see Mondory as Rodrigue.' If Racine
ever watched *La Mort de Sénèque*, the best French play about
Nero's court before his own, he would probably do so, not
because of either its subject or its author but because Madeleine
Béjart was outstanding in the part of Epicharis, a woman
tortured by Nero. Let your mind dwell for a moment on
this remarkable woman, who taught Molière how to run a
theatrical company, and whose acting both he and Racine
may have watched at the same time.

This is not to say that we may forget the critics. The playwrights certainly could not. Their individual importance may have been exaggerated: hardly any of them could or did write a play. And we know what authors think of people who prescribe in theory for what is much harder to produce in fact. But the attitude these critics stood for was more important than any of them were. Even Corneille had to take that seriously. Within a few years of *Britannicus*, society salons were to listen to the most vigorous of these critics, Boileau giving in neat verse what the keenest minds of the day thought about drama. And no doubt basically Corneille and Racine not only took such views seriously but agreed with them. They agreed, that is, on the fact that the pleasure of the dramatic spectacle depends on its form, on the smoothness of presentation. They tried to avoid anything that would disturb the harmony of the spectacle, to avoid rough lines, low or prosaic language, unlikely events, too great strain on people's imagination. They tried to supply, and the public obviously wanted them to supply, plays which were regular rather than riotous, which did not distract an audience by change of theme or place or time, but which tended to concentrate the attention on a single, general, basic and maybe well-known subject. If we may go by La Bruyère, the better kind of spectator enjoyed this concentration that took him completely out of himself: you will find his words closely pertinent to the play we are studying:

Le poème tragique vous serre le cœur dès son commencement, vous laisse à peine dans tout son progrès la liberté de respirer...

3. Sources

I hope that enough has been said to give you at least a
rough idea of the medium in which Racine was working. It
is fatal, to your own pleasure no less than to good scholarship,
to think of his work only academically, as if he set out to
write a 'classical' play. He wrote for money, and in com-
petition. His first and perhaps hardest problem was therefore
to find a theme, either new and unknown on the stage, or
one that he could renew and not merely copy from someone
else. *Britannicus* is one of the most original works in the
French language, but Racine was not original in putting
Roman history, or even the Emperor Nero, on the stage.
Corneille had only a few years before written a play about the
Emperor Otho, one of Nero's favourites, later exiled. Gilbert
had treated the same period in 1660. More remarkable than
either was Tristan's play I have already mentioned, produced
in 1644. All these could have been seen or read by Racine;
any of them may have helped him to focus his subject. But
there is really no doubt where he got that subject from. As
he admitted, he owed it to one of his favourite authors,
Tacitus:

A la vérité j'avais travaillé sur des modèles qui m'avaient
extrêmement soutenu dans la peinture que je voulais faire
de la cour d'Agrippine et de Néron. J'avais copié mes
personnages d'après le plus grand peintre de l'antiquité, je
veux dire d'après Tacite. Et j'étais alors si rempli de la
lecture de cet excellent historien, qu'il n'y a presque pas un
trait éclatant dans ma tragédie dont il ne m'ait donné
l'idée. J'avais voulu mettre dans ce recueil un extrait des
plus beaux endroits que j'ai tâché d'imiter, mais j'ai trouvé

que cet extrait tiendrait presque autant de place que la tragédie.

This seems a clear statement, yet this is just where the mis-understandings begin. What Racine owed to Tacitus is not an easy matter to determine; it is far more complicated than his mention of a list of purple passages would suggest. I think that you will not go far wrong if you keep in mind three quite separate points. They look more pedantic when separated but it is better to be clear, where our textbooks may lead us astray. The first fact is that Racine was a passionate reader of Tacitus. The second is that the Roman historian suggested the setting and the general theme of Racine's play. The third is that Racine's actual subject is not in Tacitus at all. I will take these points in order, so that you may skip or consult as you wish.

We must remember that Racine was what to-day we should call something of a classical scholar. He read his Greek and Latin classics not only easily but intensively. Most of our reading material did not exist for 17th-century readers: no newspapers, no magazines, little fiction or modern biography. If you go to Cambridge and look round the library of Samuel Pepys, a well-read English contemporary, you will be struck by this. You will see the classics, translations of the classics, a certain amount of travel, a lot of religious literature, and poetry. Books were in fact more rare and precious then than now. They were read with more intensity. And Racine was a natural reader, who loved ancient books and whose powerful imagination led him to visualise what he read. His son has left us a description of how once, long after he had stopped play-writing, he picked up his Sophocles and read a passage aloud with such feeling that everyone in the room, including himself, seemed carried away. It is thus that he would read Tacitus to himself. The Latin which for us is a stumbling-block was for him an adornment. To recover something of his impression we should read, in modern English (as Professor Grant allows us to do in his new Penguin translation), the two chapters containing the facts used in the play (that is Chapters 10 and 11, 'The Mother of Nero' and 'The Fall of Agrippina').

In these chapters we may find the main borrowing of Racine for his play. He found in Tacitus a picture of the young Emperor Nero becoming ever more restive of the powerful personality of his mother. Let us imagine him reading such sentences as these:

> From this moment the country was transformed. Complete obedience was accorded to a woman, and not a woman like Messalina who toyed with national affairs to satisfy her appetites. This was a rigorous, almost masculine despotism. In public Agrippina was austere and often arrogant. Her private life was chaste, unless power was to be gained. Her passion to acquire money was unbounded. She wanted it as a stepping-stone to supremacy. (p. 246)
>
> . . . Agrippina also enhanced her own status. She entered the Capitol in a carriage. This distinction, traditionally reserved for priests and sacred objects, increased the reverence felt for a woman who to this day remains unique as the daughter of a great commander and the sister, wife and mother of emperors.   (p. 261)

If you will look at line 156 of your play you will see that the poet was so impressed by this last expression that he has retained it, but in a quite different context. He has not used the living detail about the carriage. What then is the actual procedure he followed? We could (and I suggest that you do so) make quite a list of names and incidents and remarks that he has picked out, so much so that we might say that what happens in his play is largely suggested by Tacitus, that its characters (with the exception of Junie) are found in his 'source'.

What is not in Tacitus

Yet it is just here that the study of sources usually stops and where it should become most interesting. 'With the exception of Junie' . . . but that is an enormous exception; without her Racine's action would be fragmentary, his play would fall to pieces. If you look closely you will see that the play is quite different in all sorts of ways from the source. Tacitus writes history, Racine writes tragedy. The effect of the first is multiple, a sense almost of a moving screen, passing figures, uncertainty. The effect of the second is absorbing, a single picture being brought closer and closer to you. The first is full of drama, of all sorts and kinds. The second is full of drama also, but filed down to a tragic concentration on the fate of a few people, almost on to a single point of conflict. To say that Racine took his tragedy from Tacitus is nearly meaningless. There are a hundred tragic subjects in those two chapters of Tacitus. Tacitus is full of other things: policy, war, social matter. Why did Racine not use these? Presumably because he wanted something else, something for which he had to force Tacitus out of context, warp his facts, force them to a new mould. What made him do this? What idea had he in mind to follow? What made him take what he took and

leave the rest? (From a mass of facts he took really very few.)
If we knew the answer to these questions we should know
how great art is made. We can guess at them in a fragmentary
way by close study of both texts. Such study can be quite
absorbing and will show us much more in the play than we
thought was there.

Clearly, Racine was not interested in the large canvas of
Tacitus. He neglects the British war, Caractacus, Mithridates,
Germany, vivid pictures that Shakespeare would have taken
into his own. Racine is concerned with a few things done by
a few people, and those not the most interesting to the
general reader. He is interested in the pale figure of Britannicus, and particularly in the events surrounding his death. It
is clear why he chose his title: he writes about what might be
called the Britannicus episode in Nero's career. Yet there is
not enough on this episode in Tacitus to fill out a play, and
even some of what there is was no use to the French poet. As
if he had other things in mind, Racine gives Britannicus a
lover, unknown to Tacitus. He gives him a servant, unknown
to Tacitus. The name Narcisse is indeed in Tacitus, and with
the character he has in the play, but he is an ex-slave of
Claudius, whose feud with Agrippina drove him to suicide,
long before Britannicus became important. (Penguin trans.,
p. 274.) Not only so, but Racine uses both these characters
as links between Nero and Britannicus. Both want the lady,
both confide in the servant. Is not this a rather significant
pointer to Racine's real subject? That subject might be the
rivalry of the two princes for one girl. But Racine makes it
clear that he has something more than that in mind. The
struggle of Britannicus and Nero is never a struggle on equal

terms. Nero has the whip hand. The question is whether he will use his full power: to do so would be to leave the path of morality and he is clearly reluctant to go so far.

Is this subject, in fact, in Tacitus at all? I cannot find it. Another pointer: in Tacitus politics loom large, in Racine they are secondary. All Racine's characters are interested in each other: Nero in his mother's love of domineering and in Junie's indifference and in Britannicus as a rival, but not for Rome so much as for Junie. His counsellors are interested in making him take directly contrary paths, but Racine did not find that opposition in Tacitus either. Consider this passage:

> When the new year came Nero ceased delaying his long-meditated crime. As his reign became longer he grew bolder. Beside she loved Poppea more every day. While Agrippina lived Poppea saw no hope of his divorcing Octavia and marrying her. So Poppea nagged and mocked him incessantly. (p. 302)

We can see what has happened. Racine has taken the fact of Nero in love, changed the lady and even the lady's action: in his play it is mother who does the nagging. This is not a dramatising of Tacitus; this seems to be the result of something suggested by a reading of Tacitus, which the French poet has preferred to develop on his own. Consequently we must look very carefully at other features of the play, for instance the character of Nero himself. Is that also suggested by Tacitus, or is it a new creation discovered and achieved by Racine? This will take us beyond the study of sources into the analysis of the play itself, where we may well make some discoveries.

4. Content

This is the point perhaps at which you should set to work.
Rather than accept my results, make your own analysis of
the play, with Tacitus at hand for reference. For the moment,
neglect the poetry and tabulate the information given to you
in the four scenes of the first Act, in the three main scenes of
the second. As you do this you will, I think, get the impression
that in the first Act you are being *told* things, in the second
you are *shown* the chief actors of the tragedy at work. In the
first we hear about Nero from the three most important
people who associate with him; in the second we are shown
the Emperor as powerful, sensual, and cruel. The groundwork
of the drama is now clear before us. It concerns the same
people of whom Tacitus tells us, but only a few of them,
and in only one kind of situation. Its main references are to
matters which are found in Tacitus, but embedded in him.
We must look both at what Racine has taken and at what he
has neglected, if we would discover the principle of his play.
Here is a typical passage:

The senate decided many matters. They forbade advo-
cates to receive fees or gifts. They excused quaestors-
designate from the obligation to hold gladiatorial displays.
Agrippina objected to this as a reversal of Claudius's
legislation. Yet it was carried—although the meeting was
convened in the Palatine, and a door built at the back so
that she could stand behind a curtain unseen, and listen.
Again, when an Armenian delegation was pleading before
Nero, she was just going to mount the emperor's dais and
sit beside him. Everyone was stupefied. But Seneca in-

structed Nero to advance and meet his mother. This show
of filial dutifulness averted the scandal.

(Penguin Classics, p. 276)

Clearly Racine read this paragraph with care. He has made
two borrowings from it, which account for nearly half
Agrippina's speech (88–114). He has neglected the material
about the senate, and, most important of all, he has transposed the incident of the Empress listening in on the senate
meeting: in his verse it appears as if she did this habitually
and as if she were the unseen inspiration of that august body.
You will find other passages in Tacitus that suggest the same
thing: that Racine has left more than he has taken. War,
politics, society; Tacitus gives space to these things, Racine
did not seem to need them. He seems only interested in people
and plots in so far as they may shed light on the duel between
Nero and his mother. His Act III, for example, is full of that
duel. The Emperor gives sharp orders to Burrhus, Agrippina
and Britannicus fight back, the former by plotting and the
latter by violent altercation; this last provided Racine with
one of the most dramatic scenes in the play (III, 8).

As a matter of fact, Racine has told us, in his first preface,
what he was doing. He was giving a private view, so to
speak, of the Emperor: 'Néron est ici dans son particulier et
dans sa famille.' Act IV surely supports this impression. Hard
things have been said about the immense scene (IV, 2), where
Agrippina produces so many facts (from Tacitus) that it has
been called by tired students 'the history lesson'. Why this
apparently dull historical catalogue of crime at what should
be the tense part of the play? Look closer and you will see
that it is neither dull, nor historical: it is dramatic. The

interview has been long sought by the one, and long avoided
by the other. Her arguments, if true, are crushing; every one of
these political facts is brought in for a personal reason, to
show how much she has done for her son, therefore how
grateful he should be. 1196 is the heart of the argument:

> Voilà tous mes forfaits. En voici le salaire.

She becomes more eloquent than ever; the insults pile up:
injures, affront, ingrat...jusqu'à ma liberté, etc. Tacitus has
supplied the material but he never showed her presenting her
whole case with this vigour and finality. Why is the scene so
dramatic? Because the real actor is the person who has to
listen to her tirade. Napoleon once complimented Talma on
the way he acted Nero in this very scene. Talma apparently
showed his growing exasperation by plucking at his imperial
gown. Racine may have learnt something, not from Tacitus
here but from a contemporary. Only five years earlier he may
have watched on Molière's stage a dissolute son listening to
the scolding of an irate parent. Néron may owe something to
Don Juan. Though rude (1224), the young man has a case
(1230, 1251), but this evokes so passionate an outburst that
he seems to give in and give up; he asks for precise demands
and grants them all. We are astonished at this volte-face, as
is Burrhus, until we learn with him in Scene 3 that Agrippina
has done her work all too well and by her persistence ensured
if not her own ruin that of Britannicus. Your analysis of this
tremendous Act does not stop here. There are two more
scenes—a double test, as it were, of Nero's will—the good
counsellor tries with near success, to keep his master on the
right road. Nero's evil genius, even more successfully, urges
him at last to be a man and to take a decision for himself.

So we come to the central 'event' of the play, right at its end. Here is how Tacitus related it:

> It was the custom for young imperial princes to eat with other noblemen's children of the same age at a special, less luxurious table before the eyes of their relations: that is where Britannicus dined. A selected servant habitually tasted his food and drink. But the murderers thought of a way of leaving this custom intact without giving themselves away by a double death. Britannicus was handed a harmless drink. The taster had tasted it; but Britannicus found it too hot, and refused it. Then cold water containing the poison was added. Speechless, his whole body convulsed, he instantly ceased to breathe.
>
> His companions were horrified. Some, uncomprehending, fled. Others, understanding better, remained rooted in their places, staring at Nero. He still lay back unconcernedly, and he remarked that this often happened to epileptics; that Britannicus had been one since infancy; soon his sight and consciousness would return. Agrippina realised that her last support was gone . . . After a short silence the banquet continued.
>
> (Penguin Classics, p. 281)

How much has Racine copied from this 'source'? Very little. He has described the event, and transposed it completely. He mentions a feast (1484) but uses no details save a poisoned loving-cup. Tacitus has given him the historical fact; he has had to alter the circumstances. Why? Presumably because they would not fit the 'idea' on which he made his play. Can we not now see what that idea was? Notice how the play keeps a spotlight on Nero and in particular on his decisions, on his loves and hates and on the way he comes to feel that he cannot escape his mother's interference. This is

surely what Racine's play is about. It would be incorrect to
call it a dramatised version of even a chapter of Tacitus. It
seems, again, to be a poetic subject suggested by a reading of
Tacitus. To know what that subject was, we have looked at
the order and content of scenes; we have discovered that they
concentrate on a private Nero, on the struggle with his
mother, on the motives behind his first independent decisions.

Before we leave this point let us remember that the play
is not the only evidence. Suppose the poet planned it otherwise than it now is. Would not his revision be a valuable
pointer as to his real design? This is in fact the case. We have
the text of two scenes at first written into the play, and later
removed. One of them is a violent dialogue between Burrhus
and Narcisse, in which the soldier appeals to the freedman to
save the soul of the Emperor. The second is an interchange,
after the murder, between Nero and Junie. Read these two
scenes for yourself and imagine what made the poet write,
and then reject, them. Remember that the playwright's job,
reduced to brass tacks so to speak, was to invent and fill some
thirty or forty conversations. These had to convey the
dramatic illusion so forcefully that critics could not say they
were untrue to what was known of the subject of the play.
Here we have what Racine rejected as 'bad shots'. Were they
written to fill out the contemporary picture, to make the
minor characters more alive? Their removal is easier to understand: without them the play is more concentrated, the
impression more unified. They fill out the Roman scene,
possibly they add some realistic touches to the aftermath of
the murder. But they could be spared. It looks as if Racine
had reminded himself that he could not afford rest-scenes,

that his subject was not Rome, nor the murder, but what we
have called the Britannicus episode in Nero's career, as an
illustration of the factors that force a man out of indecision.
He is a weak man in a powerful position (perhaps the better
case therefore for watching influences play upon him and
clash with each other). Would you not say that something like
this seems to be Racine's real subject? Just as *Macbeth*, which
looks like a feudal story, has been called a poetic statement
about evil, might we not say that *Britannicus*, which at first
sight looks like two chapters of Tacitus, is a poetic statement
about the mystery surrounding decision?

Perhaps we have solved our problem too quickly, for in
looking closely at what is presented to us in this play we have
missed out what for many of its admirers is an essential factor.
That is its form. In a classical play the form shows the subject.
It is not the icing on the cake, it *is* the cake. So let us look
at the form.

5. Form

If we could really use our eyes, we should see that the form
is the most obvious thing, literally, about a play: what it looks
like. Look at the play, not the people or the arguments. What
does it look like? Not prose, for it is all in verse. Not Shakespeare, for it has few characters and no rough speech or
physical action. Now if the subject had been the murder of
Britannicus would not Shakespearian realistic prose have been
the effective medium? The converse of this is that if Racine
has gone to the extreme to avoid prose and realism it is
because his subject is not one that lends itself to prosaic portrayal. Racine's subject allows only *description* of seduction

that another dramatic convention would have encouraged him to *represent*. Yet, as so often, his 'récit' is more dramatic than actual representation might have been. (These lines, 385–398, are worth your study; they have been much admired.)

The basic element of dramatic form in a play is the words themselves. Have you ever looked closely at these? Count up the realistic expressions: you will find them few and colourless: just enough to suggest things like look, gesture, emotion. Hardly any objects are described in this poetry. A recent investigation says that the poet is not even interested in the human body: 'Les personnages de Racine sont à peu près dépourvus de réalité physique. Le poète nous apprend qu'ils pleurent, qu'ils pâlissent, qu'ils rougissent, mais cela veut dire seulement qu'ils souffrent, qu'ils ont peur, qu'ils éprouvent de la honte.' (J. G. Cahen: *Le Vocabulaire de Racine*, 1946, p. 46.) Now look at the first words of the play: 's'abandonne au sommeil, attendre son réveil, errant dans le palais, appartement, assuré, déclaré, chaque jour, à mon tour...' How would you describe this vocabulary? The words seem select, dignified, the reverse of common or everyday words. Yet line 5 is a prosaic, and even modern, request. This is part of an illusion that works upon us from the first line to the last.

The words are uttered in lines, of set length and set to rhyme in couples. These, as we all know, are called alexandrines, the classic French measure, that gives to the trained French listener the chief delight of the play, but not easy for English readers, who do not hear them well recited, to appreciate. So their effect is lost on too many of us. This is partly because we imagine that they should be read or scanned like English blank verse, divided into bars and feet. In French verse there is no such regular alternance of stress. There is a fixed number of syllables to each line. Since the rhymes are alternately masculine and feminine, the latter have the extra feminine *e* sound (escort-*e*, port-*e*). This sound is always *heard* except at the end of the line or before another vowel. To read French verse as prose is to ruin it. Thus in lines 10 and 11 the actor will say cess-*e*, fair-*e* (in the second case, but *fair* in the first); in line 13 he will say *gène* as one syllable but *chaque* as two, in 14 *importune* as three.

In each full line there is a main stress which usually comes after the sixth syllable. Since this divides the line exactly in half, English writers have been very rude about it, comparing it to a pump-handle, and to a mackerel split down the back. The French feel no monotony, because within each half-line there is a minor stress, which the poet shifts at will; it may occur on any one of the six syllables, thus giving five different ways of saying each half-line (called in the books hemistich). Another way of putting it would be to say that the French poets like to write the alexandrine in two equal groups of syllables. (As a matter of fact our usual breath group is nearer six than twelve syllables. Try this by reading aloud a line or two of Bossuet and you will find that your voice is saying groups of five, six or seven syllables at a time.) So that any alexandrine couplet could just as well be called four lines of six syllables as two lines of twelve. Once you grasp this you will get much more pleasure from the reading, so play about with lines until you get used to marking the major and minor stresses.

Thus line 349 is clearly divided into two equal parts. It would be silly to read it otherwise than stopping at the

comma. Now look at the two parts your voice has separated.
They are not merely of equal length but of exactly similar
structure: each consists of a verb, an object and the same
possessive pronoun; six words in all, each of which has its
counterpart in the other half of the line. Savour the pleasure
of reading, and still more declaiming, this. You will find that
your voice is naturally accentuating the two verbs and, as in
prose, the last syllable of the stem: examine, observe. So your
voice is dividing the first hemistich into two groups of sound,
say 3 plus 3. The natural division of the second half-line is
almost but not quite the same, 2 plus 4. Imagine that this line
began 'remarque leurs regards', the meaning would be the
same, the parallel would be even more exact with the grouping in the second half-line; it would be monotonous. The use
of examine instead of remarque makes all the difference to
the euphony. Now look at the next line in the same way.
There, too, is a natural pause in the middle at attendre. But
your voice will make minor pauses, I think, after the first
syllable and after the ninth, thus

Vois | si j'en puis attendr(e) || un fidè | le secours.

You have in fact read line 349 with this grouping: 3, 3, 2, 4,
and line 350 with this grouping: 1, 5, 3, 3.

You will find that line 351 has this grouping: 2, 4, 2, 4, and
352 this: 4, 2, 3, 3. The examples you hunt up for yourself
will soon show you why the French think us crazy to call the
alexandrine a monotonous measure in the hands of Racine or
Corneille or Hugo or Verlaine or Valéry. Racine is not tied
down even to this scheme. He will invert the major and the
minor stresses and divide his line into two groups of 3 plus 9

(line 360). To read line 371 as 6 plus 6 is far less effective than to read it as 2 plus 10, with a minor stress on the sixth syllable. Line 381 may be read as easily in three parts (the so-called *vers ternaire* which the Romantics affected) as in four.

Now what does all this mean, and why should busy people be concerned with marking syllables? It means that a main feature of the formal presentation of Racinian tragedy to you and me is rhythmical diction, speech that delights us by its sound, and rhyme, and balance, and contrast. We may as English people think that is waste time if the result is to be unnatural, something unlike real speech, suggesting something unlike real life. But a great poet knows what he is doing. He was just as well aware of this as any of us are. He says to us in effect: allow me to create something for you, something that seems far away from your daily life. In the end, if you accept my convention, you will be surprised, and pleased, and you will see the point. Louis Jouvet was not old-fashioned or pedantic and he used to say that we miss the whole point of a play if we do not yield to its illusion, its deliberate falsity, because 'dans le théâtre on commence par le brillant, le faux, le simulacre, pour aller à une vie intérieure'.

Once you have grasped that the verse is a flexible instrument, notice how Racine can use it to convey varied forms of statement. Line 191 reads just like prose, and there are many like this. Yet the one before it is as euphonious and suggestive a grouping of sounds as words can make. His use of the middle division of the line is masterly. It can convey two short statements that suggest all kinds of conflict and contrast; very often they suggest the underlying tragic conflict of the whole play. Study lines 87–90 in order to see how they emphasise, and express (without explanation), the deep cause of the woman's fear: outward respect from her son, but inner mistrust; more honours, less influence; presents, which have the ironical effect of estranging rather than endearing. An American critic can help you here:

> The verse itself realises in every detail the action of the whole . . . In the perfect balance of the rhymed couplet, in the perfect balance of the individual line (regularly though not invariably broken in the middle) one feels the logical form of thesis and antithesis, the tragic split between reason and passion . . .
>
> (F. Fergusson, *The Idea of a Theater*, p. 66)

Consider your play as a drama of echoes. As one half of a line may answer the other, so one speech caps another, in the formal sense of antiphonal reciting; so also one scene echoes another. The cruelty of II, 6, for instance, is foreshadowed and alluded to in Scene 3. Scene 6 is itself a good example of the multiple perspective of Racinian drama. The action that we watch is merely, but most poetically, someone watching someone else. It has been compared to the Hall of Mirrors at Versailles, where everybody is both observed and observing. Here, in case you do not get the point, the young lover is watched most anxiously by his lady; both are watched by the unseen Nero who has arranged it all:

> Madame, en le voyant, songez que je vous vois.

But in an even truer sense it is the poet who has arranged the complete spectacle, that we should watch the Emperor watching his victims. In such a situation the pleasure and quality of the poetry lies in the fact that the lines have a double meaning:

Vous êtes en des lieux tout pleins de sa puissance
Ces murs mêmes Seigneur peuvent avoir des yeux...

Strictly these lines have three meanings: one for Britannicus, who is puzzled and ignorant of the real situation, another for Junie and Nero, who both know what is going on, and yet another for us who are being given the scene as a spectacle of which Nero is not, as he thinks, in command. To say that walls have ears is not poetic, except when they really do, and when the victim is the only one not to know that they do. And not only is the single line ambiguous, half of it, a hemistich, may recall something in violent conflict with the suggestion of the other half. Are not 750–751 of this kind?

'...Mais je mettrai ma joie' gives a glimpse of sadism,
'...à le désespérer' suggests the pitiless fate in store for the powerless victim.

Even more so 'Je me fais de sa peine', a casual reference to what we know to be anguish, followed within the line by '...une image charmante' where the adjective has not the modern meaning, but recalls sorcery: all that Junie's pain means to Nero is a literally fascinating picture that he cannot dismiss from his mind, but that inspires no pity at all in him.

Racine is unique in achieving these gems of concentration. Many of his lines are as condensed as the epigrams of his contemporary La Rochefoucauld. Perhaps one more case may stand for many (line 756):

'Fais-lui payer bien cher' suggests (but how vaguely and gently) the penalty; 'un bonheur' is the young man's sole crime, and 'qu'il ignore' suggests the irony of the fact that he does not know his offending.

This veiled suggestiveness of the expressions is a part of the form of the play and very easy for the new reader to miss. The speech even of criminals in this drama is polite, calculated not to give offence, not to be realistic but only slightly suggestive. Cruelty is conveyed by irony and offset by politeness: 'Caché près de ces lieux je vous verrai, Madame...' suggests a most cruel design, but the expression is in terms of contemporary French courtesy (lines 573–602 give a lengthy example of this use). The important thing for us is to see that the French poet is suggesting two things where an English dramatist might be content to render a single impression, a Roman incident as Tacitus reveals it. But a Roman incident in 17th-century terms is either a hopeless misfit or a very subtle dramatic convention. In this play it is clearly the latter. One never gets the impression of clumsy or rough writing; all is harmonious, elegant, dignified, intentional. The value of this particular convention is that it suggests to reader or spectator two situations at once, his own as well as one removed in time and place. For this reason all is veiled, things are understated. The genius of French classical art, said André Gide, is *la litote*, understatement. This feature of Racinian form is rarely discussed, yet vital to full enjoyment of any of his plays. Notice how few Roman events are precisely described, how many are the general allusions to qualities, that is to things that are with us now, as much as they could ever have been to Romans. The vision given by this chastened style is not the actual and active world of Tacitus; it is a vague vision of a moral jungle, where we may watch the weakness and beastliness of men, in safety (as we can in any play, because however real it seems we know it is not real enough to harm us), at a distance and in perspective. Tragedy is perhaps the greatest achievement of French classical art because it found a means of expressing the otherwise inexpressible, the skeletons that we could not look upon except when transmuted by art. (Perhaps you should read again the opening lines of Canto III of Boileau's *Art Poétique*.)

6. Characters in Conflict

Let us now stop looking at examples of how Racine puts things and return to the question of the main emphasis in his play. Drama implies conflict; Racinian drama offers us cases of acute conflict. What exactly in *Britannicus* is the conflict? What exactly are the contending forces? We have seen that, as the poet said, the tragedy was suggested to him by Tacitus. Of the many tragic subjects in that vivid author, Racine has picked out one, has filled it out by pursuing one set of suggestions and neglecting many others, by transposing here and inventing there. He does not impose the Roman scene upon us: he suggests it in such a way that attitudes, often quite modern attitudes, are in his play as vivid as actions, in fact attitudes *are* his actions. As if he were telling us by the very vagueness of the details not to limit our interest to the historical figure but to see them as pattern of many situations, as suggesting modern situations no less than ancient. If we look closely at what is offered us, all the conflicts of his play seem summed up in the opposition of two characters, Nero and his mother. We do not need Racine's preface to tell us that these were the protagonists of his play. Let us see in greater detail how these are presented.

A poet well read in Tacitus could not fail to be struck with the commanding figure of Agrippina, powerful, intriguing, unscrupulous. He shows her in her decline given up to outbursts of rage and scoldings of her son. She is suspicious of his presents, in particular of that costly jewelled garment that he went out of his way to send her:

> But Agrippina instead of regarding this as an addition to her wardrobe, declared that her son was doling out to her a mere fraction of what he owed her—all else but this one thing was kept from her. Some put a sinister construction on her words. (Penguin trans., p. 279)

or again

> Agrippina was alarmed. Her talk became angry and menacing. She let the Emperor hear her say that Britannicus was grown up and was the true and worthy heir of his father's supreme position, now held, she added, by an adopted intruder who used it to maltreat his mother. Unshrinkingly she disclosed every blot on that ill-fated family, without sparing her own marriage and her poisoning of her husband . . . This worried Nero . . . As the day of Britannicus's fourteenth birthday approached, he pondered on his mother's violent behaviour . . . (279–80)

This happened in A.D. 55. As Nero becomes eager to murder his mother, so she becomes the more passionate to retain power, and four years later we hear this:

> Finally he concluded that wherever Agrippina was she was intolerable. He decided to kill her. His only doubt was whether to employ poison or the dagger or violence of some kind. Poison was the first choice. But a death at the emperor's table would not look fortuitous after Britannicus had died there . . . (p. 303)

It is this desperate antagonism that Racine has put into his play, not as Tacitus reported it, for he did not need, or use, the event of the mother's death. He used the violence of clash that Tacitus assumes and suggests: Agrippina desperate to keep power, Nero equally determined to win independence. (As to why this single moment was all that Racine wanted must be left for further discussion.) Yet what a change in presentation of the same kind of person. Racine transposes her deeds into an attitude, an attitude more pathetic than political. She rants and plots (but not much or not prominently in the play) but above all she invokes the past, she fears the future and her own vanishing authority: 'L'ombre seule m'en reste.' 'Je m'assure un port dans la tempête.' All that Racine tells us of her points this feature of a woman despairing of her escaping son, seeking every chance to recall the past, worried about the *balance* of power, her own word (259). She is a sort of 'lion devenu vieux'. If psychology is what we are looking for, Racine's picture is more simple, generalised, sublimated, than that of Tacitus, who has the complexity of the great historian.

Turning to the other main figure, I leave you to conduct the detailed comparison. You will find it fascinating. Tacitus is far more daring, outspoken, brutal than Racine. There is nothing in the French play about Nero's orgies, open violence on the street, unnatural vices. Vice is suggested only by single remarks showing heartlessness, lack of sensitivity, callous disregard of others, and of the truth. But on the surface, as we noted, there is politeness, courtesy, some charm, intelligence. Racine's Nero is no Roman, but (like his costume) a mixture, an elegant, enigmatic figure, with a good record so far, with scruples, not so much a bad man as a weak man, or not yet a man, unused to full power, weak enough to believe the person he has talked to last. Curious contrasts are suggested: he is naïve, and ironical, brutal and yet refined, dictatorial, yet uneasy and afraid. A man who might turn out either way, depending on his surroundings, a man of wax taking the imprint of his advisers. It is as if Racine were showing the paradox of a weak man in a position of power; the figure is not unlike the Caligula of M. Camus.

In a way Racine has been too successful in putting this fascinating figure at the centre of his play, as he was later to be with Phèdre. Both plays have been read as studies of a single character. In comparing them you will probably find that this is not fair to their creator. Thésée, like Agrippina, is an essential part of the poet's picture. M. Lanson, to whom teachers owe so much, compares at length Racine's interpretation of Nero with that of Renan, as if both were interesting and valid readings of history. For M. Faguet

le rôle de Néron est la plus prodigieuse peinture psychologique que je connaisse. Dans cette journée de vingt-quatre heures, de dix peut-être, l'auteur a si bien pris ses mesures que tout Néron passe devant nos yeux, depuis l'enfant vicieux et lâche qui tremble devant sa mère en s'excitant à la braver, depuis l'amoureux sensuel mêlé de despote méchant qui adore les pleurs qu'il fait couler, depuis l'histrion vaniteux et fat qu'on pousse au crime en humiliant son amour-propre d'artiste, jusqu'à l'assassin hypocrite et froid qui tue en souriant, jusqu'au parricide tranquille qui rêve le meurtre de sa mère en laissant tomber sur elle, nonchalamment, quelques mots d'ironie glacée. On s'étonne que tant de choses, et j'en oublie, aient pu tenir en cinq actes.

(E. Faguet, *Drame ancien, drame moderne*, p. 210)

This is worth your translation and analysis, but do you not think that these scholars are mistaking the part for the whole, one opponent for the two-sided conflict that Racine suggested he was very keen to represent? You have already found that Agrippina plays as big a part in the tragedy as Nero does. Do you not think that she is shown as in the end forcing *his* hand by overplaying her own? Why, according to the evidence in the play, did he commit his first crime? I think that the poet has strewn possible suggestions of an answer through his play, but that he has (no doubt intentionally) avoided any hint that crime can have a single cause. At any rate the Agrippina scenes (especially I, 1 and 2; III, 3-5; IV, 2; V, 2) are just as important as any of the Nero scenes. In a sense her scenes *are* about him, is not that the point? His first crime is not planned; he is almost dissuaded from it by Burrhus. It is the result of exasperation as well as of any plot on Nero's part. Was there any means other than crime for Nero to be free? Is it not really mother's deed rather than son's? These are questions to which every reader may give his own answer. They show, better than any professor's argument, how deep the play goes and how incorrect it may be to speak of Racine as a master of psychology. I doubt myself if any practising psychiatrist would go into ecstasies over the 'depth' of psychology in *Britannicus*. I suggest to you that it is the work of a poet rather than of a historian or a scientist, that if you are interested in it you will be interested in what a poet has imagined, not in what a student of Tacitus has copied, nor in any account of Nero as a monster. 'What's Hecuba to him or he to Hecuba?' We are interested in great dramatic characters not as men or as copies of historical figures but as centres of dramatic suggestion. *Britannicus* seems to be a historical play; it is really an imagined action, of the order and power of a novel by Hardy or Dostoievski. If you take the trouble to listen to its words, to watch its overtones and undertones, to take it as poetry in fact, you will be charmed by the imagination of its creator.

This charm seems to depend on the fact that powerful and even ugly forces are present behind what looks like a piece of history. Close reading shows us that the poet has arranged his material in such an order as to suggest those forces, never to give any direct impression of them, as modern realism would do. Cruelty is here, deception is here, treachery is here, but conveyed to us as it were without their sting, recognisable still but clothed in language of grace and elegance and rhythm. This process would seem to make the play less a play, to soften the dramatic shock. But this is the reverse of what happens. The play is full of drama, of a kind that does not issue in blows and screams, but deeply and essentially violent. The feeling of clash and conflict is conveyed by the first main argument of the play (I, 1 and 2). The words of Agrippina suggest resentment far deeper than its occasion. She is angry, not only because she cannot have access to the Emperor when she will, but because that fact is a symbol of her fading power. She is restless, and anxious to recover the past. She constantly refers to the way things used to be and fears the way things are going to be. She resists, not Burrhus only, not Nero only, but Time, loss of power, the more bitter because she once had all power: she was in fact the architect of the situation that now threatens her peace of mind, her ambition, her life. Notice how even the terms used, the lines, the expressions balance one another and suggest clashing elements, unavoidable changes, widening chasms. Nero is in command now, increasingly: 'impatient' is a stronger word than it has since become. So impatient that she must feel 'importune'. This bitter reversal of fortune is Agrippina's main, almost her sole, theme. She wants to put the clock back, to the time when she had influence instead of, as now, deference. She wants 'un peu moins de respect, et plus de confiance'. She is exasperated because 'Je vois mes honneurs croître, et tomber mon crédit.' She is determined to pursue the power that is passing from her, to recover the dominance of mother over son, while all the time the son become Emperor strives to achieve independence by keeping her as a subject. The fact, the regret, the striving, all this is suggested in line after line, very often both positions are put within a single line (as in 88 and 90 quoted above). In Racinian drama single lines, half-lines, convey deep antagonisms. Thus in 123:

Mais je le poursuivrai d'autant plus qu'il m'évite

conveys nothing concrete or outwardly startling; an unpractised reader may easily miss its point; we have all done so, many times. But the balance must be intentional: the balance of 'poursuivre' and 'éviter' makes the line. Not only balance, but paradox. It is a pointless chase, in which the one pursues as the other escapes. In later years, and no doubt unwittingly, the poet came again upon the same relationship of pursuit and evasion and gave it even more perfect expression, as he applied it to God pursuing man, in his conscience (a sort of 17th-century version of the *Hound of Heaven*):

Je l'évite partout, partout il me poursuit.

(*Athalie*, 489)

This, I suggest, is something of what it means to read
Racine, to be alive to the contrasts and the clashes, the more
poetic for being deep-seated rather than on the surface of
speech. Looking at the structure of this play you will find that
the big scenes seem to be so arranged that each major actor
has a single decisive meeting with each of the other three,
in the course of which the essential cleavage between them
is dramatically expressed. The two minor characters, the
advisers, are brought in for consultation apparently when a
main character is desperate or forced to make a decision.
Thus Agrippina has two interviews with Burrhus (I, 2;
III, 3), Nero two with Narcisse (II, 2; IV, 4). The main weight
of the play seems to rest on three interviews, all of them
involving the central character, Nero. I refer to his scene with
Junie (II, 3), to his scene with Britannicus (III, 8) and to his
scene with his mother (IV, 2). I think you will find that the
chief features of Nero's personality and role that the poet
wishes us to notice he has stressed in these three scenes. All
three are worth careful analysis that I have no space for here,
and that you will do more successfully on your own. Yet
none of them gives us the impression that the dramatist wishes
first and foremost to evoke before us a particular psychology,
of a tyrant or a criminal. Each of them brings out a dramatic
clash. The first seems to me a marvel. Nero does not make
love to Junie; he pays court to her, and gives her, in polite
terms, to understand that she must belong to him and re-
nounce her lover. There is a faint suggestion of lust; behind
the compliments there seems to be cruelty, cold and planned.
But these are suggestions of which we are free to make what
we will. What we should not miss is the emergence of a

tense dramatic situation, condensed in 669 and 670, nothing spectacular to look at, but theatrical for all that, and in the only way that declaimed, rhetorical, drama could be theatrical, by staging a scene in which the proprieties were preserved but violence was done. Of this kind of effect it would be difficult to think of a more dramatic example than what happens in II, 6: the scheme devised and expressed by Nero to the victim in II, 3. It allows Racine to achieve an effect as pathetic and tense as Pyrrhus' threat to kill Andromaque's child unless she submit to him. Even the terms of the ultimatum are similar: compare with 690 *Andromaque*:

> Madame, en l'embrassant, songez à le sauver.

Notice how often in this play a dramatic conflict is brought to the point of a sharp interchange, that either splits the alexandrine or produces contrasting lines. Thus, between Narcisse and Nero:

> Quoi donc? Qui vous arrête
> Seigneur? — Tout:...
>
> (460–461)

Again, between Nero and Junie:

> Et quel est donc, Seigneur, cet époux? — Moi, Madame.
> (572)

Yet again, between Junie and Britannicus:

> Parlez, nous sommes seuls...
> — Vous êtes en des lieux tout pleins de sa puissance.
> (709, 712)

Or between Agrippina and Burrhus:

> Je confesserai tout, exils, assassinats,
> Poison même. — Madame, ils ne vous croiront pas.

Only when you have sought out these dramatic clashes can you hope to find the true dramatic centre of the play. I have suggested to you that it is not a presentation of the murder of Britannicus nor of the jealousy of Agrippina, but that there would seem to be a desire on the part of the poet to portray both these things as factors in the emergence of Nero as a person. As Emperor he must decide. He cannot do so, for not only is he clearly by nature irresolute but he 'wants it both ways'. He wants Junie, which means that he must deal with her lover, and incur his mother's wrath. He wants freedom at last from Agrippina, yet can only get free, as Narcisse is clever and quick to show, by an act, a murder, in fact a crime. His independence and his crime are bound up together.

This only becomes clear to him, I think, after the tremendous tirades of his mother. It is not the least dramatic surprise in this play that the interview most desired by Agrippina is precisely the one that turns the scale against all that she wants. By her tactless and ambitious scolding she converts her son . . . to a crime that will lead to others.

In what sense does this make a tragic spectacle? That is perhaps the most difficult question of all to answer. For myself (and none of us need adopt what anyone else says in this matter) I feel that I am watching in *Britannicus* the sort of tragedy that Corneille had achieved in *Horace*, the tragedy that springs from irreconcilable personal attitudes. Between the fire-eater and the pacifist there can in the last resort be no compromise. The triumph of the one is a scandal to the other. This I watch in *Horace*. Similarly between two generations insistent on domination there can be no more than temporary understanding. If a Nero and an Agrippina are both out to win, at any cost, with no holds barred, no scruples observed, no bonds sacred, then it is more than a struggle for power, it is a struggle for life and death. Any true picture of such a struggle will involve ultimate violence. Secure behind the protective screen of the form he has chosen, Racine can suggest all the ultimates that in actual portrayal would horrify: lust, seduction, threats, poison, death. His play gives a true picture of certain possibilities in our human nature. As M. Picard has written of it:

> L'action est une des plus violentes et des plus inhumaines que Racine ait imaginées. On sent assez l'horreur de ce combat pour une toute-puissance mauvaise, entre une mère et son fils, également effrénés.

Yes, we feel the horror, but we are not horrified. Why is this? Is not the conflict of evil imagined at such a deep level that the actors seem like puppets, hardly responsible for their acts, still less so for the consequences? The main actor is so weak, so obviously the battleground for all the conflicts, that he evokes pity. As Racine has put the matter he can hardly be blamed. Like the poet's later creation, Phèdre, he is consumed in the struggle: he does not die in this play, but he has achieved mastery over enemies only at the cost of becoming little more than a beast. The final impression perhaps is not of any single purpose, but of a moral tempest that burns up those who get involved. So Giraudoux, himself a poet and a playwright, compared it to our *Wuthering Heights*: 'L'orage est moins pitoyable sur les Hauts de Hurlevent. Racine a trouvé l'altitude parfaite de la tragédie.'

For Further Reading

BY RACINE

The most pleasant and useful edition of the plays is that of Pierre Mélèse for the *Collection Nationale des Classiques Français*, 5 vols., 1951. (Volume II contains *Britannicus*, and also a contemporary pamphlet on the play.) Single plays are presented from the actor's point of view in the *Editions du Seuil*: M. Barrault's *Phèdre* is outstanding. Scholarly material is found in R. C. Knight's *Phèdre* (Manchester U.P., 1943) and G. Rudler's *Mithridate* (Blackwell, 1943). Racine's notes on the Poetics of Aristotle have been edited by E. Vinaver (Manchester U.P., 1944).

ON RACINE

François Mauriac has written a poetic *Vie de Jean Racine*. The best recent work of reference is R. Picard: *La Carrière de J. R.* (Gallimard, 1956). Subjective elements are studied by R. Jasinski: *Vers le vrai Racine* (2 vols., Colin, 1958). On the aesthetics of the plays the best general work is by T. Maulnier: *Racine* (Gallimard, 1936.) Lytton Strachey has an excellent essay in *Books and Characters*.